www.dinobibi.com

Author: Belinda Briggs
Editor: Kristy Elam
Illustrator: Teena Rahim

© Copyright 2020 - Dinobibi: All rights reserved. No part of this publication may be reproduced, stored in retrieval systems, or transmitted by any means, including electronic, mechanical, photocopying, or otherwise, without prior written permission of the publisher and copyright holder. **Disclaimer:** Although the author and Dinobibi have taken all reasonable care in preparing this book, we make no warranty about the accuracy or completeness of its content and, to the maximum extent permitted, disclaim all liability arising from its use.

# CONTENTS

Introduction (pg. 4)

Geography (pg. 6)

Weather (pg. 14)

History (pg. 16)

Culture and Tradition (pg. 23)

Native Plants and Animals (pg. 31)

Famous People (pg. 38)

Major Cities and Attractions (pg. 41)

# INTRODUCTION: HELLO FRIENDS!

Hi, my dear friends! Welcome to one of the most beautiful countries on the Asian continent, Thailand.

My name is Boonsri, and I am an 11-year-old girl living with my parents in Bangkok, the capital city of Thailand. Bangkok is a bustling, modern city in which you will find modern skyscrapers alongside historical well-preserved and well-maintained monuments. More about me later! Tell me about yourself.

What is your name? Does it have any special meaning? Just to let you know, my name is pronounced Boon-see, and it means 'beautiful.'

Which country are you from?

How did you travel to Thailand? By plane/ship/any other mode of transport?

What are your expectations from your Thailand trip?

Who are you traveling with? Please write down their names and their relation to you.

Ok, now that you have told me so much about you, I will tell you about me and my family. I am an only child which makes me lonely sometimes. But I have a large group of friends in school and in the community where I live, and it makes up for not having a sibling.

I go to a school in my neighborhood, and my mom teaches math for secondary school students there. My dad runs his own restaurant serving delicious Thai food that both locals and foreign visitors love.

Kids in Thailand attend elementary school and then can go on to do secondary or high school and college after that. Our parents have to pay for our education although there are government schools that offer free basic education for children up to grade 9. All male students are required to attend military training while in high school.

# CHAPTER I
# GEOGRAPHY OF THAILAND

Located at the center of southeast Asia, Thailand is one of the most beautiful countries in the region with a rich cultural and historical heritage. Thailand borders are as follows:

- Myanmar and the Andaman Sea to the west

- The Mekong River separates Thailand from Laos in the northeast

- The Dongrak Mountain range separates the country from Cambodia in the southeast.

- Malaysia and the Gulf of Thailand is to the south of Thailand

### Fun Fact
Before 1939, Thailand used to be called Siam.

Thailand covers an area of approximately 514,000 square kilometers (about 198,000 square miles) which is about as big as Spain.

Thailand also has coastal islands, and some of the largest ones include Phuket, Phangan, and Samui.

### Pop Quiz!

Can you name the capital of Thailand?

1. Bangkok
2. Phi Phi Islands
3. Cambodia

(Answer — 1. Bangkok)

# The Four Geographical Regions of Thailand

The map of Thailand looks like the head of an elephant with the trunk part extending southward along the Malaysian border. This part of the country is famous for its thick rainforests, beaches, and limestone formations.

The forehead part of the elephant's head, which is to the northwest of the country, consists of misty, green mountains. The highest peaks of this region are at a height of over 2000 meters (about 6500 feet).

The ear part forms the border with Cambodia and in this region, which makes up 1/3rd of the country's area, you will find the Khorat Plateau. The northeast part of Thailand houses the majestic and mighty Mekong River. The central part of Thailand, where Bangkok is also located, has another mighty river, the Chao Phraya River.

The entire country of Thailand can be divided into four geographical regions including the North, South, Center, and the Northeast.

**Central Thailand** — Surrounded by plateaus and mountains, Central Thailand consists of paddy fields that are irrigated by the Chao Phraya River and its several tributaries. With vast plain lands, warm weather, plentiful water from rivers and canals, and great soil conditions, Central Thailand is perfect for cultivation and is one of the most productive agricultural regions in the world.

Several major rivers of the country flow through Central Thailand, and some of these rivers include Chao Phraya, Tha Chin, Mae Klong, Bang Pakong, and Pasak. As this region is home to many rivers, it is also prone to flooding.

**Northern Thailand** — The temperatures in Northern Thailand are cooler than the rest of the country. You will find beautiful, green mountains, thick, misty jungles, and fertile valleys here. The customs of the people living here are quite different from those living in the southern parts of Thailand. Many hill tribes occupy this area of Thailand.

As Northern Thailand is mostly mountainous, it is the place that most of the country's rivers and streams originate including the majestic Chao Phraya River. This region is also great for crop cultivation, especially wet rice cultivation. Like in most countries, the forest area here has reduced in size due to deforestation.

Panoramic view of Nong Pak Chee grassland in Khao Yai National Park in Thailand

**Northeast Thailand** — Known as Isan or Isaan in the Thai language, Northeast Thailand is home to the vast Khorat Plateau, rolling farmlands, mountains, and national parks. This part is the least visited and traveled section of the country, but many seasoned travelers believe that Northeast Thailand is the most interesting and authentic part of Thailand.

The lakes on the Khorat Plateau are mostly drained by the Mekong River. During the monsoons (which lasts for a short while), heavy rainfall is also seen which could result in flooding too. But, mostly, Northeast Thailand has long, dry spells and is prone to droughts so much of the land has sparse grasslands.

Also, as the soil is thin and not very fertile, farming is poor. Much of the sticky rice varieties, especially the jasmine variety for which Thailand is famous, are cultivated here. While agriculture does not thrive here as much as it does in Central Thailand, the green grass is highly suitable for cattle rearing.

**South Thailand** - South Thailand is a short, narrow isthmus that borders Malaysia. South Thailand is famously touristy because it is home to stunning islands and beaches. You can see beautiful Thai islands on both sides of South Thailand; on the Gulf of Thailand in the east and the Andaman Sea on the west.

This region also has marvelous limestone formations and ruins of great ancient cities that were influenced by thriving cultures in Sumatra, Cambodia, and Java. The region is rich in minerals like tin and gypsum. The agricultural products of South Thailand are rubber and coconut.

# Rivers and Lakes of Thailand

**Mekong River** — With a length of 2700 miles, the Mekong River is one of the largest of the world. Originating from the Tibetan Plateau, which is over 16000 feet high, it flows through six nations including China, Myanmar, Laos, Thailand, Cambodia, and Vietnam before emptying into the South China Sea.

Father Gaspar da Cruz of Portugal was the first European to describe the entire journey of this gorgeous river. In Thailand, it flows through the east and north parts of the country and plays a critical role in the economic activity of six provinces of the country.

Mekong River

People living along this river are farmers and fishermen. During the months of May and June, the water level increases which, in turn, brings in an abundance of fish supply. The Mekong River is not just a source of water and fishing for the Thais but is also a divine aspect of their lives.

**Fun Fact**
The Thai name of Mekong River is Mae Nam Khing.

**Chao Phraya River**— The Chao Phraya river system is the largest in Thailand constituting nearly 35% of the nation's land area and is the most important source of water in the country.

Aerial view of the Bangkok city skyline and the Chao Phraya River

Today, the 370-km (229 miles) long Chao Phraya River is one of the most vital transportation links in Central Thailand, especially to ship teak and rice to Bangkok. Since ancient times, the Thais have made their homes along the banks of this beautiful river which is considered to be the bloodline of Thailand and its people.

Also, the banks of the Chao Phraya are home to multiple colorful festivals including Songkran, or the Thai New Year, and Loi Krathong which is celebrated in November every year to give thanks to the water god. Visitors can take boat rides and enjoy the stunning views of Bangkok while floating on this wonderful river.

This river originates in the district of Pak Nam Pho in Nakhon Sawan Province where four rivers, the Ping, Nan, Yom, and Wang, converge to form an estuary. The vast river then flows in the southward direction passing through various cities and towns including Bangkok before emptying into the Gulf of Thailand.

**Cheow Lan Lake** — Also known as the Khao Sok Lake, the Cheow Lan (sometimes spelled 'Larn') lies amid ancient rainforests in the Surat Thani Province. This lake has some unique forms of accommodation, such as floating hotels, for visitors!

Cheow Lan Lake limestone cliffs, Khao Sok National Park, Thailand

The Cheow Lan Lake lies within the Khao Sok National Park, and its emerald green waters add to the greenery of the surrounding forests. The forests of the Khao Sok National Park are believed to be older than the Amazonian rainforests. The lake is home to a variety of freshwater fish and is an important source of food for the birds of the national park.

The Cheow Lan Lake was formed when a dam for hydroelectricity was built on the Pasaeng River which resulted in the flooding of five villages. Of course, all the people from these villages were evacuated and resettled elsewhere before the flooding happened.

## Bueng Boraphet Lake

Bueng Boraphet is the biggest freshwater lake in Thailand. In fact, thanks to its large size, this lake is known as the 'Great Lake' or 'Northern Sea. Located in the Nakhon Sawan Province, this beautiful lake was originally a wetland which was dammed up in 1930 resulting in the formation of the lake.

Songkhla Lake

## Tha Chin River

The Tha Chin River branches out from Chao Phraya River in Chai Nat Province. This river has multiple names including Makham Thao River, Suphan River, and Nakhon Chai Si River. The Tha Chin River is 439 km (272 miles) long and is divided into three sub-basins all of which irrigate paddy fields.

**Songkhla Lake** — Located in the south of Thailand in the Malay Peninsula, the Songkhla is the largest natural lake in the country covering an area of about 1040 square kilometers (about 401 square miles). The endangered Irrawaddy dolphin species can be found in this lake.

The lake drains into the Gulf of Thailand through a wide strait in the city of Songkhla. The most beautiful part is the 75 kilometers (about 46 miles) long spit (a narrow area of land) that separates the lake from the sea. People around the lake depend on it for their livelihood through fishing, tourism, cattle-rearing, etc.

*Sunrise scene of two pagodas on the top of Inthanon mountain in Doi Inthanon National Park*

## Mountains of Thailand

**Doi Inthanon** — Located in Chiang Mai Province and at a height of 2565 meters (about 8400 feet), Doi Inthanon is the tallest mountain peak in Thailand. You can either hike or drive to the top of this popular tourist attraction.

If you are physically fit, then you can take the help of a local guide and hike up the mountain. The places to see there are the Royal Twin Pagodas, the highest point in Thailand, Suriphum Waterfall, and the stunning vistas of the green forests.

Other important mountain peaks in Thailand include:

- Khao Mokoju
- Phu Lang Ka
- Doi Chiang Dao

### Fun Fact

In addition to the belief that Thailand has some of the best and gorgeous sandy beaches in the world, it is home to some of the most beautiful mountain peaks as well. The tallest mountain peak in Thailand is Doi Inthanon.

# The National Flag of Thailand

The national flag of Thailand is called Thong Trairong which translates to 'tricolor.' The flag has five horizontal stripes with the following colors from top to bottom: red, white, blue, white, red. The central blue band is twice as wide as the other bands on the flag.

The red stripes symbolize the blood spilled by people who fought to maintain the nation's independence.

The white stripes stand for Buddhism (which is the main religion of the country) and purity.

The blue stripe represents the monarchy of Thailand. The blue also stands for solidarity towards the country's World War I allies including Russia, France, Great Britain, and the USA. The flags of all these countries also have red, blue, and white in them.

## Other National Symbols of Thailand

National animal — The elephant

National anthem - Phleng Chat Thai which literally translates to 'national anthem'

Languages spoken — Thai and English

National bird — Siamese Fireback Pheasant

Coat of arms — Open-winged Garuda, a mythical half-bird-half-man creature from Hindu and Buddhist mythology

National sport — Muay Thai, a martial art

National tree — Golden shower tree

# Currency of Thailand

The currency of Thailand is baht, and its international symbol is THB. Here are some interesting facts about money in Thailand:

- The currency notes carry the image of the Thai monarch. Therefore, putting them in your back pocket is not allowed because it means you are sitting on the king's image!

- Stepping on currency notes and coins is considered to be an act of offense against the king.

- The currency denominations of the Thai baht are 1, 2, 5, and 10 (as coins) and 20, 50, 100, 500, and 1000 (in notes/bills).

- In rural areas, small currency notes and coins are displayed in the shops as a mark of respect towards the king.

Here is the cost of various everyday items in Thailand:

Regular milk (1 liter) THB55

A pair of name-brand jeans THB1800

A dozen eggs THB50

A loaf of white bread THB38

# CHAPTER 2
# WEATHER IN THAILAND

Phu Chi Dao mountain in Chiang Rai province, Thailand

Being only 15 degrees from the equator, Thailand has a tropical climate. However, the entire country is spread across 16 degrees of latitude which results in varying climate conditions in different parts of the nation. Different climates across the country mean there are multiple things to do during the varying seasons.

Officially, Thailand has three seasons including hot, cold (or cool), and wet seasons. Usually, the rainy season lasts for 6 months, the hot season lasts for 3 months, and the cold season (dry and relatively cool temperatures) lasts for 3 months.

## The Hot Season

The hot season in Thailand happens from February-March to May-June with April and May being the hottest months. Temperatures during the hot season can go up to 85F or sometimes even more. The hot season is also a very dry season with very little or no rain in most parts of the country. In fact, in the northeast part of the country, people could be affected by drought too. In the south of Thailand, however, there is a lot of rainfall during the hot season.

## The Monsoon Season

The wet, or monsoon, season can vary across the country but usually lasts from May to October. In the west side of the isthmus part of the country, monsoons can begin as early as April or May. In the south part of Thailand, monsoons can last even up to November. But, mostly, the monsoons last from June to October. During this time, the temperatures cool down considerably.

The rains are not constant during the wet seasons. Typically, you will see heavy or sometimes even torrential downpours for about an hour or two each day after which there is a dry spell. Rainfall is the heaviest towards the end of the monsoon season. If you are visiting Thailand during the monsoon, it is best for you to carry an umbrella or a raincoat in your handbag.

The monsoon seasons in Thailand are primarily influenced by the Northeast and Southwest monsoon winds.

## The Cold Season

The cold season typically lasts from November to February. However, even during these months, the weather might feel hot or warm to many visitors. The average temperature in Bangkok during the cold season hovers at around 75F during the day and about 65F at night.

For about three weeks in December, nearly all parts of Thailand experience unusually cool weather. This cold snap is especially felt in the north and the northeast of the country. The further south you travel, the cold months are a bit warmer than in the north.

In some parts of northern Thailand, like in Chiang Rai and Chiang Mai, the cold season could get chilly enough for frost to form. The locals usually like to travel to the north of the country during the cold season to experience the chilly weather.

# CHAPTER 3
# HISTORY OF THAILAND

People have been living in Thailand for thousands of years. Let us look at the history of this wonderful nation.

## Early History

Around the 9th century B.C., the Khmer and the Mon people established kingdoms in areas that form present-day Thailand. The culture, society, religion, and politics of these people were influenced by existing South Asian civilizations including Cambodia, India, Malaysia, Laos, and Vietnam. The Thais maintained trade contacts with the people of these regions. Merchants and traders had to pass through the routes controlled by the Mon and Khmer people.

### Prehistoric Thailand

Archeologists and history experts have been able to ascertain that Thailand has been populated since the Paleolithic Age which is about 20,000 years ago. Archeologists have dug up bronze tools and weapons from the Khorat Plateau they believe to be from around 3000 B.C. They also have evidence that rice was cultivated in this place since 4 B.C.

**The later part of Thailand history can be divided into the following important eras:**

### Nanchao Period – 650 A.D to 1250 A.D.

During this period, Nanchao, which is a region located in the southwestern border of China's Tang Empire, was a buffer between Thailand and China. The original people of Nanchao were called the Tai, and they migrated to Southeast Asian regions, including Thailand, for many centuries in the first millennium A.D.

### Sukhothai Period – 1238 A.D. to 1438 A.D.

In 1238, Sri Intraditya, a Tai chieftain, declared his independence from the ruler of Khmer and founded a kingdom at Sukhothai in Central Thailand in the Chao Phraya Valley. The people of this new kingdom took on the name of 'Thai,' which translates to 'free,' to distinguish themselves from the people who were still under the Khmer rule.

The Kingdom of Sukhothai took control of the Isthmus of Kra in the 13th century and was able to collect tributes from different vassal states including Myanmar, Vietnam, Laos, and the Malay Peninsula.

Vassal states are those kingdoms that promise allegiance to a higher authority (in this case, the Sukhothai Kingdom) in return for safety and protection. The vassal states were required to pay tribute to the kingdom that ruled over them.Slowly, the Sukhothai lost its power, and by 1438, it was completely subjugated by a new dynasty called Ayutthaya.

## Ayutthaya Period – 1350 A.D. to 1767 A.D.

The Ayutthaya Kingdom was founded in 1351 and lasted until 1767. Around 1360, Buddhism became the official religion of this kingdom, and a legal code was set up that combined Buddhist and Hindu philosophies. This legal code was in force until the end of the 19th century in Thailand.

The Ayutthaya Kingdom's superiority in the Asian region grew by leaps and bounds, and soon, the Khmer Kingdom was subdued. While the king was the absolute ruler, the rest of the region was divided into small principalities that were governed and ruled by different kings who owed their allegiances to the monarch at Ayutthaya.

During this period, Thailand became highly influential and prosperous socially, economically, and politically. At the beginning of the 16th century, Ayutthaya entered into trade relations with the Portuguese, and by the end of that century, it was also trading with the Dutch people. In the 17th century, Ayutthaya set up trade relations with England and Japan.

However, as the Europeans began to demand more rights for themselves through the use of military force, the Thais started anti-European movements and protests in fear of losing their original identity and culture to Western influences. Ayutthaya consciously alienated itself from the West for about 150 years from the late 17th century. Learning, art, and literature flourished in the country during this time.

In 1767, Myanmar attacked the capital and destroyed it which resulted in the downfall of the Ayutthaya Kingdom. However, the subjugation of Thailand to Myanmar did not take place because Myanmar itself was attacked by the Chinese.

### Pop Quiz!

Can you guess the name of the Indian city which is connected to Ayutthaya?

1. Ayodhya
2. Delhi
3. Mumbai

(Answer – 1. Ayodhya; this is the capital city of the kingdom of Rama, the hero of the famous Hindu epic, Ramayana)

## Early Chakri Period – 1782 A.D. to 1868 A.D.

The Chakri Dynasty was established in 1782, and during this period, two important things happened:

1. The king's court moved to Bangkok across the Chao Phraya River.
2. The art and monuments destroyed during the Myanmar invasion were restored in Ayutthaya.

The former glory of Thailand was slowly restored, and the capital was shifted entirely to Bangkok. The isolation of the west came to an end, trade treaties were signed with the British and the US, and territorial expansions were stopped in 1851.

King Rama IV, who ruled Thailand from 1851 to 1868, learned from the mistakes of the Chinese and Burmese who suffered defeats at the hands of the British which ended in being forced to sign unjust and unequal treaty terms. This king chose to negotiate with the European powers without going to battle and signed highly favorable trade treaties with France, Britain, and the US.

In 1855, King Rama IV gave the name of Siam to his kingdom. Before this, the regions covering present-day Thailand were known by the name of the capital city. He also brought in excellent administrative and legal reforms to Siam helping in its growth and development. But, his death in 1868 halted further reforms in the country.

## Chulalongkorn Period — 1868 A.D. to 1932 A.D.

While King Rama IV laid the foundation for various reforms in Siam (as it was known then), during the reign of King Rama V the effects of these reforms were felt. Moreover, King Rama V continued the reformatory progress and included judiciary, finance, and political reforms as well to his agenda.

He abolished slavery, introduced tax reforms, and established a regular army. In 1893, he established a central administration to replace provincial self-governing bodies, and set up European-style schools and education systems.

In 1897, the country saw the first railway line built between Bangkok and Ayutthaya and between 1901 and 1909, eventually this railroad was extended even further north. In the southward direction too, railroads were built connecting Thailand to British railway lines in Malaya.

During this period, the French and British started establishing their colonies all over Southeast Asia which threatened the independence of Siam. In return for their sovereignty, the Thais relinquished their territorial claims over Cambodia, some of the northern states of Malaya, and Laos.

Despite its territories being reduced, Siam protected its independence from European colonization. In fact, Siam became a buffer state between French and British colonies. Siam joined the Allies in World War I and sent its troops to battle for Britain and France. These actions resulted in increased favorable trade treaties with these two European countries. Additionally, Siam was one of the founder members of the League of Nations, the precursor to the United Nations.

Passenger train for Bangkok departs from Ayutthaya station

## Constitutional Government — 1932 A.D. to 1941 A.D.

In 1932, the monarchy in Thailand came to an end, and a constitutional government was established although the monarch is still the Head of State. The first parliamentary election in Thailand was held in 1933. In 1939, the country was named Thailand or 'Land of the Free.'

In a bid to encourage local businesses, foreign companies were taxed heavily, and local companies were given a lot of tax exemptions and subsidies.

**Fun Fact**
The Thai name of Thailand is Muang Thai!

# Thailand During World War II and After

The government in Thailand was conflicted during WWII with some officials, including the Prime Minister Phibun, aligning with the Japanese, and a few other officials aligning with the Allies. However, when the Allies bombed Bangkok during the war, both strong public protests and powerful anti-Japanese political leaders forced Prime Minister Phibun out of office.

After the war, the country set up a bicameral legislature consisting of a lower house elected by the people and an upper house elected by the members of the lower house. Again, Siam became the official name of the country in 1946 which also witnessed a general election. After some bitter disputes between the newly elected prime minister and the royal family, the former resigned and left the country.

### Fun Fact

This movement of power between military and civilian governments continues even today with the constitution being rewritten multiple times. Thailand has had 17 constitutions in its history.

Bhumibol Adulyadej Rama IX portrait

King Rama IX (King Bhumibol Adulyadej) was crowned the new king in 1951, military rule under Prime Minister Phibun was re-established, and Siam was again called Thailand. In 1968, a new constitutional government was set up and National Assembly Elections were held in February 1969. But in 1971, military rule was again set up as the civilian government could not manage the multiple problems threatening the sovereignty of Thailand.

In 1973, people started protesting against the strict military regimen. On October 13, 1973, 250,000 demonstrators came out on the streets to protest against the military government resulting in army troops opening fire. King Bhumibol took unprecedented direct action and forced the cabinet to resign, and the military dictatorship was brought to an end.

# The Thailand Monarchy

**Fun Fact**
Chakri dynasty is the present ruling royal house of Thailand.

Although the government in Thailand has moved between civilian to military many times, the basic structure remains the same and consists of the executive, legislature, and judiciary. The king holds sovereign power over all the three branches of the government. And even if the constitution of Thailand limits the powers of the king, he still wields considerable influence over the running of the government.

The law of the land states that the throne of Thailand passes on from father to son only. Only males are allowed to ascend the throne in my country.

## Seven Great Kings of Thailand

Seven great kings are revered as the best in the history of Thailand, and their statues were erected in the Royal Memorial Park in 2015 to honor them. Let me give you a brief insight into each of these seven kings who are revered by the Thais.

**Fun Fact**
King Ramkhamhaeng also hold the moniker of "Father of the Thai language."

King Ramkhamhaeng Monument, Sukhothai, Thailand

### King Ramkhamhaeng the Great

He belonged to the Sukhothai Period, and his reign lasted from 1279 – 1298 A.D. He is famous for creating the Thai alphabet and writing system in the country. King Ramkhamhaeng the Great was also responsible for making Theravada Buddhism as the official state religion of Thailand.

### King Naresuan the Great

He ruled during the Ayutthaya period from 1590 – 1605 A.D. Even as a Crown Prince, he freed Ayutthaya from Burmese (Myanmar) control. He is also known for setting up trade relations with the western countries bringing economic growth and prosperity to Ayutthaya. In fact, he strengthened his kingdom so strongly that no one dared attack it.

### King Narai the Great

Also of the Ayutthaya Period, King Narai ruled from 1656 – 1688 A.D. He was a great poet, and Thai literature and art flourished under his reign. He adopted a friendly approach to the Europeans and signed plenty of trade agreements with them which enhanced the economic strength of his kingdom.

### King Taksin the Great

He was part of a Thonburi Period which lasted for a short while between the Ayutthaya and the Early Chakri Period ruling Thailand from 1767 – 1782 A.D. When Ayutthaya fell to Myanmar in 1767, King Taksin the Great fought hard to drive out the invaders and then reunited Thailand. He is most famous for rallying the nationalism of Thailand during a particularly tricky crisis when the country ran the risk of being completely controlled by the Burmese.

### King Buddha Yodfa Chulalok the Great

He was the founder of the Chakri Dynasty and took on the title of King Rama I. He moved the capital from Ayutthaya to Bangkok. His primary achievement was to bring order into the administrative chaos Thailand fell into after the fall of Ayutthaya. The Buddhist scripture, Tripitaka, was revised under his watchful eyes.

### Fun Fact

The present King of Thailand is Maha Vajiralongkorn, also known as King Rama X.

### King Mongkut

His official title was King Rama IV and before ascending the throne, he spent 27 years as a monk in a Buddhist monastery. He was the first king of Thailand to learn the English language and enter trade relations with Europeans. He was an avid learner and keenly studied many western subjects of science with astronomy being his favorite.

*Chulalongkorn Rama V portrait*

### King Chulalongkorn the Great

Also known as King Rama V, he is, perhaps, the most respected king of the Chakri dynasty. He ruled from 1868 – 1910 A.D., and during his 42-year reign, Thailand made great advances. He abolished slavery, promoted modern education by setting up the Department of Education for the first time in Thailand and did a lot of work to modernize his beloved country. Under his rule, the first railroad track in Thailand was built. His death day, October 23, is a government holiday even today.

*Wat Phra Singh, Buddhist temple in Chiang Mai*

## Religion in Thailand

The only strict religious law in Thailand is that the king must be a Buddhist. Other than that, everyone is free to follow any religion as there is no official state religion in present-day Thailand. However, nearly 95% of Thais are Theravada Buddhists, and the rest follow Christianity, Islam, and Hinduism.

Although Buddhism is Thailand is essentially of the Theravada form (a particular sect of Buddhism), the Thais have adopted Chinese beliefs along with local nature worship also. The Buddhist temples in my country are beautiful, to say the least with golden statues, tall domes, and spectacular architecture.

Thailand is also called as the 'Land of Buddhism,' and this religion is so prominently followed here that it is a tradition for men to become monks before they turn 20 even if only for a short period. Typically, men choose to become monks for a period of three months before getting back to normal life. Thailand has two Buddhist universities and more than 35,000 Buddhist temples.

Muslim Thais are found all over the country with the biggest concentration in the southern parts of Thailand. Hindus constitute only 1% of the population, and yet, this religion influences a lot of Buddhist culture and traditions. Many Buddhists in Thailand worship Hindu deities even today. Christianity was established in my country way back in the 1550s when Christian missionaries from Europe came to spread their religion.

### Pop Quiz!

What is the Thai name for a Buddhist temple or monastery?

1. Wat
2. Wok
3. Temple

(Answer – 1. Wat)

# CHAPTER 4
# CULTURE AND TRADITION

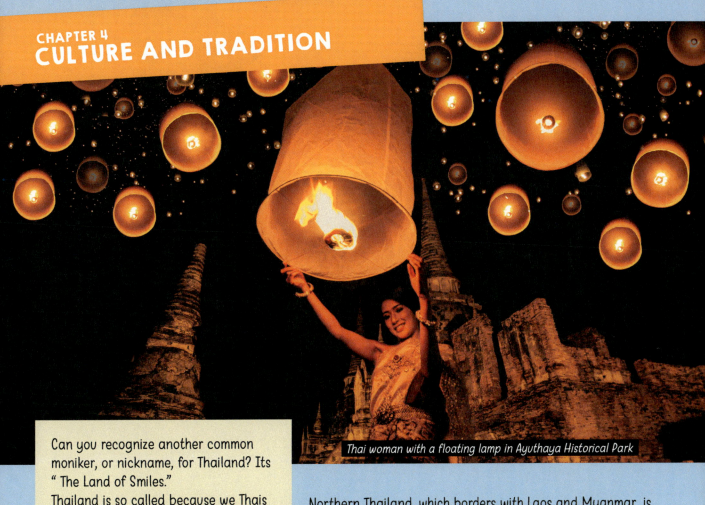

*Thai woman with a floating lamp in Ayuthaya Historical Park*

Can you recognize another common moniker, or nickname, for Thailand? Its "The Land of Smiles."
Thailand is so called because we Thais are very friendly and hospitable people who welcome visitors with smiles.

Northern Thailand, which borders with Laos and Myanmar, is heavily influenced by Burmese culture. The northeastern part is more or less isolated from the rest of the country and is populated by a Lao-speaking majority. The people here lead an agricultural way of life.

Southern parts of Thailand are typically home to many fishing communities that influence the local culture. Central Thailand is home to Bangkok and has a vibrant cosmopolitan culture but is deeply rooted in Buddhism. Central Thailand is the economic, financial, and political center of the country.

The culture in Thailand is deeply influenced by religion, specifically Buddhism. Additionally, we have cultural influences from neighboring Asian countries like China, Myanmar, Cambodia, Vietnam, Malaysia, Laos, and India. The culture of Thailand can be divided into four distinct forms aligning with the four geographical regions.

## Wai

Greeting in Thai culture is done through a gesture called 'Wai.' Place your hands together as if you are praying, raise them to your face, and lower your head slightly as if in a bow.

The higher you raise your hand the more elevated the other's person's status is. For example, to greet a peer, you only need to raise your folded hands to your chest whereas if you are greeting an elderly person, then you must raise your folded hands to your nose. Greeting a monk calls for raising your hands even higher, and the monk is not required to return your greeting.

## Interesting Facts about Muay Thai

Traditional Muay Thai fighters

Muay Thai, a form of martial art, is the national sport of my country. Some interesting facts about this fascinating sport:

- It originated in the medieval period as a form of hand-to-hand combat for use by soldiers in battles.

- Muay Thai uses eight 'weapons' including two each of fists, elbows, knees, and legs.

- Muay Thai practitioners use hand wraps (like boxing gloves) to protect their knuckles as well as to stabilize their wrists.

- Some matches are considered sacred.

# Other Interesting Facts about Thailand Culture

Standing above an image of Buddha or the king is also considered a discourteous act.

We Thais have a unique and, to some foreigners, a strange way of letting the host know that we enjoyed the meal. We leave behind a spoonful or two of the meal because an empty plate means there wasn't enough food and the leftover part means we are completely satiated and full!

We do not stop ON the threshold of the door of any home. We step OVER it because we believe that spirits live on the threshold and stepping on it is considered disrespectful to the spirits.

Public displays of emotions are frowned upon. We are taught to control our anger and present ourselves in a positive light at all times even under challenging circumstances.

## Fun Fact

The three-wheeled vehicle that is a common mode of transportation in Thailand is named after the sound of the engine- "tuk tuk."

# National Holidays in Thailand

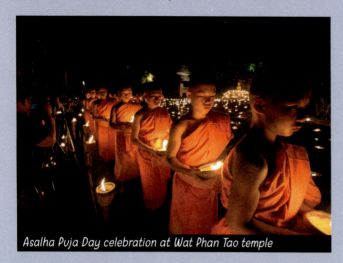
Asalha Puja Day celebration at Wat Phan Tao temple

**Asahna Bucha Day** — Also known as Asalha Puja Day, this day commemorates the Four Nobel Truths preached by Buddha. These four noble truths include dukkha (suffering), tanha (desire), Nibbana, or Nirvana, (salvation), and the eight-fold path. Understanding these four noble truths is critical to understanding Buddhism.

The Asahna Bucha Day falls on the first full moon of the eighth lunar month and typically in the first fortnight of July. On this day, people visit temples, leave gifts of flowers and candles for the monks, and take their blessings. Men who choose to follow monkhood even temporarily start on this auspicious day.

## Chinese New Year

In Thailand, only some provinces (those with a high concentration of Chinese population) declare a holiday for Chinese New Year which is also called Spring Festival or Lunar New Year. The holiday is on the first day of the first month of the lunar calendar falling typically between late January and mid-February.

## Chakri Day

The Chakri Day is celebrated on April 6 every year to commemorate the establishment of the Chakri Dynasty which still rules Thailand and also to remember and honor all the great kings of Thailand.

The Haka lion is dancing in Chinese New Year celebration in Thailand.

## Christmas

Christmas Day is a declared holiday only in certain provinces of the country. However, the delightful sights and sounds of Christmas are clearly visible all across the country. At tourist venues and hotels, people don the costume of Santa Claus. Traditional Christmas dinners are hosted by hotels and restaurants.

## Chulalongkorn Day

This day celebrated every year on October 23 is commemorated to the achievements of King Chulalongkorn who revitalized Thailand to fit into the modern 20th century.

Authorities offered flowers at the statue of King Rama 5 on Chulalongkorn Day.

## Constitution Day

December 10 is the Constitution Day in Thailand to remember the day in 1932 when the first constitution was adopted. Celebrations on Constitution Day include parades and processions, firework displays, representations of past and present kings and their contribution to the growth and development of the nation.

## Coronation Day

May 5 is celebrated as the Coronation Day of the King Bhumibol Adulyadej who officially ascended the throne on this day in 1950. Typically, Coronation Day is celebrated over three days:

- On Day 1 (May 3), monks gather together in the Grand Palace and perform Buddhist rituals.

- On Day 2 (May 4), the chief Buddhist monk reads out the coronation proclamation after which ceremonial incantations follow. People walk around the Temple of the Emerald Buddha thrice, and the robe of Emerald Buddha is also changed on this day.

- On Day 3 (May 5), the coronation ceremony is re-enacted. Then, the king honors various achievers from different fields.

## HM, the Queen's Birthday

The 12th of August each year is a national holiday to celebrate the birthday of the Queen of the former King Bhumibol. This day is also called the Queen Mother's Birthday as she is the mother of the present King Vajiralongkorn. It is also dubbed as Mother's Day in Thailand in honor of all mothers across the nation.

## HM, the Late King's Birthday

On 5 December every year, Thailand gets a national holiday to celebrate the birthday of the Late King Bhumibol Adulyadej. He was a pillar of stability and helped Thailand sail through smoothly during times of crisis.

## Labor Day

Labor Day in Thailand is commemorated on May 1.

**Khao Phansa Day** - The Khao Phansa Day marks the first day of Buddhist Lent; a period of sacrifice which falls during the eighth lunar month. This day is also called 'Rains Retreat' because the day falls at the beginning of the Thai rainy season and monks retreat into their monastery for intense study and meditation for three months.

> **King Vajiralongkorn's Birthday**
>
> On 28 July every year, the Thais celebrate the birthday of King Vajiralongkorn, the present monarch.

**Visakha Bucha Day** — The Visakha Bucha Day commemorates three events in Buddha's life: his birth, enlightenment, and death. Usually falling in the month of May, on this day, most Thais visit Buddhist temples to pray and seek Buddha's blessings.

**Passing of HM, the Late King**
King Bhumibol Adulyadej passed away on October 13, 2016, after a long rule of over 70 years. This day is a national holiday to commemorate his death anniversary.

**New Year's Day** - Like in all countries around the world, the New Year as per the Gregorian Calendar is celebrated on January 1 every year. This is in addition to the Buddhist New Year called Songkran which is also celebrated grandly in Thailand

*Fireworks above Bangkok on New Year's Day*

*Elephant spraying water on people at the Songkran Festival*

**Songkran Festival** — This festival marks the beginning of the Thai New Year. Typically celebrated between 13 and 16 April, Songkran is also known as water festival because washing away of negativity with water is a traditional ritual performed on this day.

**Makha Bucha Day** - Another Buddhist holiday, the Makha Bucha Day is celebrated to commemorate the day when Buddha gave speeches to his disciples who flocked to him to learn what he had to teach. This day typically falls in Feb-March every year.

**Royal Ploughing Ceremony** — Thailand observes May 13 as Royal Ploughing Ceremony day when symbolic rice planting takes place which is believed to bring about a good harvest in the coming year. Buddhist and Hindu priests bless the symbolic planting ceremony and pray for a good harvest in all of Thailand.

*The Royal Ploughing Ceremony*

## Popular Foods of Thailand

Coconut is also used extensively in our cooking. We use the water, milk, and flesh of the coconut in many of our dishes. Let me tell you some of my favorite Thai dishes:

Rice is the staple food and is included in all meals including breakfast, lunch, dinner, and even desserts. In fact, rice is so vital in Thai culture that if we are hungry, then we will say, 'I want to eat rice.'

There are two types of rice in Thailand including the regular white variety and the sticky, glutinous type which is known as sticky rice. Curries are usually combined with rice.

**Guay Teow** — Also known as noodle soup, Guay Teow is a very popular Thai dish which you find everywhere you go. It is made with noodles (obviously) to which pork, chicken, or beef is added. Sometimes, people love to add meatballs and wontons to the broth, too.

Som Tam — The origin of this dish is the Isaan region or the northeastern part of Thailand. The classic variety of Som tam is made with shredded green papaya, carrots, beans, shrimp, tomatoes, tamarind pulp, fish sauce, and a lot of chilies mixed and pounded together. It can be quite spicy, so I would suggest you start with a small portion first and see if it suits your taste before trying out more. My family and I love it! The English name for Som Tam would be green papaya salad.

**Tom Yum Goong** — Another typical Thai dish, this amazingly delicious broth is made using kafir lime leaves, lemongrass, shallots, galangal (ginger-like spicy veggie), and a generous portion of fish sauce. I love it with mushrooms and fresh prawns. If you don't like it very spicy, you can add coconut cream which will reduce the heat and also thicken the soup.

**Pad Thai** — Pad Thai is the national dish of Thailand, usually the first dish that visitors to my country like to try. This fried noodle dish is made with chicken or shrimp. You will find Pad Thai in every street corner of Thailand.

**Panang curry** — Mildly spicy, Panang curry is a favorite among foreign visitors most of whom cannot handle the high levels of spice in Thai food. It is usually served with shrimp, and sometimes with vegetables too.

**Mango and sticky rice** — This dish called Khao Niew Ma Muang in Thai is the most popular dessert in Thailand. It is made with sticky rice and mango slices with the sweetness coming from condensed milk. It is a must-try for you.

**Banana leaf and sticky rice** — Black beans, sweet coconut milk, sticky rice, and sugar are stuffed into a banana leaf which makes one of the most delicious Thai desserts.

**Sweet Thai crepe** — Sweet Thai crepes are also a favorite Thai street food. Filled with meringue and topped with egg yolk, the crepe is one of my favorite desserts.

**Mung bean candy** — Fruit-shaped candies are made using sweetened mung bean paste that is smashed and then glazed.

# CHAPTER 6
# Native Plants and Animals

## Animals of Thailand

Sprawling national parks, thick rainforests, long coastlines, and picturesque landscapes ensure that Thailand is home to a variety of flora and fauna. Let me give you a brief insight into some of the most beautiful and exotic plant and animal life found in my country.

Annual Surin Elephant Roundup in Surin, Thailand

### Elephant

What is the national animal of Thailand? Yes, it is the elephant. We love our elephants, and therefore, I must start this chapter with this graceful and majestic animal. Elephants can be found all across my country, and they are revered like royalty. Thai elephants are not only gentle but also very playful. Thailand has many elephant sanctuaries where you can interact with these wondrous creatures.

Thailand has an annual festival in which the elephants are honored. In this festival called Surin Elephant Roundup, multiple events are organized including an elephant parade at the end of which there is a huge breakfast spread for the animals to feast on.

The elephant is a symbol of Buddhism as well. People believe Queen Maya, the mother of Buddha, had a dream where an elephant appeared and gave her a white lotus before entering her womb. This dream was interpreted as the child she would give birth to would be very special.

**Tigers** – Although most the tigers in Thailand are in captivity, you can find some of them in the wild too. The number of tigers in the wild is believed to be less than 300 though forest officials think that the numbers will go up soon because the animals are seen to be breeding and giving birth to cubs.

Pangolin curled into a ball

**Pangolin** — Pangolins have hard scales all over their body, and they curl into a ball to escape from predators. However, traffickers have been able to catch pangolins to smuggle them out as they are used in China in the preparation of traditional medicines. This indiscriminate hunting of pangolins has reduced their numbers. But they can still be seen in the wild. Another name for pangolins is anteaters because ants and termites are their primary source of food.

**Fun Fact**
Pangolin will curl up into a ball to defend themselves from predators in the wild.

Binturong or bearcat on a tree

**Fun Fact**
Binturong the bearcat smells like popcorn!

**Binturong** — These animals are also called bearcats because they bear a striking resemblance to both bears and cats. However, binturongs are not related to bears or cats in any way.

These creatures use their smell to let other binturongs know that this area is taken, and they should move on and find another place.

**Bears**
Even though the number of bears in Thailand is not very high, both Asian Black Bears and the Malayan Sun Bears can be found here. You can see bears at multiple tourist places including Khao Yai and Khao Sok National Parks.

**King cobra** — You can find King cobras all over Thailand, and these reptiles are easily recognizable, especially when their hoods are raised. Wildlife experts believe that baby king cobras are more dangerous than the adult ones because they cannot control the venom they emit when they sting resulting in high doses being injected into the victim.

> **Fun Fact**
> The venom of the king cobra will most likely affect a human's nervous system.

**Gibbons** — Found in almost all the national parks of Thailand, gibbons are amazing tree-to-tree swingers. They can swing up to 15 meters (49 feet) in one leap and can achieve a swinging speed of up to 55 kph (34 mph)! They are more easily heard than seen thanks to their distinctive calls.

Lar Gibbons

Tokay Gecko

**Tokay gecko** — These beautifully colored lizards are, perhaps, the most interesting of the multiple varieties of lizards found in Thailand. They are named after their call which sounds like 'tokay.' You can hear this call right through the night in Thailand. Although they are beautiful to look at, they can give you a nasty bite if you try to handle them. So, always watch them from a safe distance.

Giant Manta Ray

**Manta rays** — If you go diving in the waters surrounding Thailand (which is a popular tourist activity), then you are quite likely to swim with these beautiful creatures. The best place to view them is around the Similan Islands off the west coast of Thailand. Manta rays come here and stay for weeks.

Some of the manta rays can grow up to 25 feet, and these large ones can eat up to 60 pounds of fish and plankton each day! These fish are sometimes called 'devilfish' because their cephalic lobes (organs attached to their heads used for capturing and eating fish) look like horns.

**Siamese crocodile** — This species is one of the most endangered species of crocodiles. They are freshwater reptiles with a wide body and a smooth snout. You can find Siamese crocodiles held in captivity in many of the national parks of Thailand. People believe the only wild ones are found in the Mekong River and some parts of Cambodia.

Siamese Crocodile

# Plant Life in Thailand

**Ratchaphruek** — Also known as the golden shower and golden tree, the small, beautiful, yellow flowers of this tree appear to tumble down from the trees resembling a 'golden shower,' hence the name. You can see these little yellow flowers all over my country; in parks, gardens, and roads, especially towards the end of the cool season when these flowers burst into blooms.

*Frangipani*

**Jasmine** — This enticingly sweet-smelling flower is a symbol of Mother's Day in my country. People believe the white color of this flower represents the gentle, pure, and unconditional love of mothers. These flowers are given as offerings to temples and even elders in the family in addition to being used as decorative flowers.

Jasmine finds its way into Thai food also as the petals are sprinkled in tea and desserts to enhance the flavor and smell of the dish. There are different species of jasmine found all over the country.

*Jasmine*

**Frangipani** — Frangipani is a decorative flower native to Thailand. This beautiful flower is used to decorate drinks, women wear it behind their ears, and as table centers. Coming in yellow, white, and pink, the frangipani is also used in religious rituals. The sweet smell of this exotic flower makes it ideal for creating excellent perfumes.

Lotus

**Lotus** — Along with the elephant, the lotus is also an important Buddhist symbol. You can find lotuses blooming in lakes, rivers, ponds, and in urns all across Thailand. The lotus is a common offering at Buddhist and Hindu temples. The lotus is not just a religious symbol but also has many other uses including:

- The seeds are a delicacy used to make delicious dishes.
- The roots are also used in cooking, especially to make soups.
- The lotus leaves are used to wrap foods before being baked or grilled.

Puple cymbidium orchids

**Orchid** — Thailand is home to over 1000 varieties of orchids and is one of the world's leading exporters of these exotic plants. You can see orchids growing in the wild as well as in orchid farms located all over the country. The wild orchids usually bloom in January and August. But you can find orchids in farms all through the year. Some of the common varieties of orchids grown and exported include denobrium, brassavola, mokara, cymbidium, and vanda.

Krachiao

**Krachiao**

These flowers blossom at the start of the monsoon season, and one of the best places to witness these beautiful blooms is in the Chaiyaphum Province in the northeast part of Thailand. Chaiyaphum is host to an annual festival where you can see these beautiful Krachiao flowers. By the way, these flowers are not related to tulips at all. They belong to the turmeric family.

### Fun Fact

Siamese lotus is another name given to this beautiful, purple flower Krachiao.

**Bat flower** — Resembling a bat in flight, these bat flowers are large and have a unique purplish-black color. The long whiskers enhance the ominous looks of the flowers which are referred to as the devil flowers. You can find bat flowers growing abundantly in the forests of Thailand. Some people believe that looking into the 'eye part' of the bat flower can bring bad luck.

**Torch ginger**

The buds of these exotic-looking, reddish-pink flowers are used in salads and the flowers themselves are used for decorations. These flowers bloom all through the year and are called torch lily, porcelain rose, red ginger lily, or wax flower.

## Major crops of Thailand

The major crops cultivated in Thailand include rice, rubber, tapioca, coconut, sugarcane, and soybeans. Jasmine rice is native to Thailand, and in fact, my country is one of the largest exporters of rice in the world. Here are some fascinating points about Thai agriculture:

- Most of the farmlands are found in the northeast and central parts of Thailand. In fact, Central Thailand is called 'bread basket' or 'rice bowl' of the country as the fertile wetlands here are great for growing crops.

- Thai farmers use strange (and many times natural) ways to protect their crops. For example, you will see scarecrows in nearly all the fields of Thailand which keep birds away. Farmers have cats to keep mice at bay.

- Some big farms use modern agricultural machinery. But many small farmers still use the old farming methods including plowing the land with the help of buffaloes.

- Large jars are kept at rice fields to catch and hold crabs that are found in the fields. The crabs are a pest for the Thai farmers because they eat paddy.

# CHAPTER 6
# FAMOUS PEOPLE OF THAILAND

Here are some of the famous people of Thailand who have made us Thais proud of their work.

### King Bhumibol Adulyadej

You already know that King Bhumibol Adulyadej was the previous Thai monarch. He was the longest reigning king ruling over Thailand for more than 70 years. Here are some fascinating and lesser-known facts about this beloved king.

- His name translates to 'strength of the land' (Bhumibol) and 'incomparable power' (Adulyadej).

- He did a lot of work to improve the state of public health of his country. This interest in the public health area was because of his parents' interests in the field. His father majored in public health at Harvard University while his mother was a nurse.

- Not only was he a great king but also a great jazz musician who could play several musical instruments including saxophone, piano, clarinet, and guitar.

- In an unfortunate car accident in 1948, the late King lost vision in his right eye. That did not stop him from becoming a skilled sailor.

- He was so loved by his people that most of the shops and homes kept his photo to honor him.

Portrait of Bhumibol Adulyadej (Rama IX)

### Angkarn Kalayanapong

Angkarn was born on 13 February 1926 in Nakhon Si Thammarat Province in Southern Thailand. He was a poet and artist, and in 1989, was named the National Artist of Thailand.

He started writing poems even as a high school student. He joined Silpakorn University to study painting. By the 1950s, he became a famous professional writer. In addition to his poetry and writings, he was famous for his paintings and drawings too.

## Thongchai Jaidee

Thailand's star golfer, Thongchai Jaidee was born on 08 November 1969 in Lopburi Province. He was a Pele fan and played football before turning to golf at the age of 16.

He was a paratrooper in the Thai Army before becoming a professional golfer at the age of 30. He says that his days in the army helped him build his physical and mental strength.

Age is just a number is perfectly reflected in his life. He is the oldest in the top 50 of the Official World Golf Ranking.

He runs a golf academy to give talented underprivileged children opportunities to identify and nurture golfing talents.

## Tammy Duckworth

Tammy Duckworth's father was an American marine and her mother was a Thai. She was born in Bangkok and then spent her childhood all over the world thanks to her father's job with the UN and international companies.

When the family moved to the US, her mother was not allowed to enter the country because she was not a US citizen. Tammy and her brother Tommy were separated from their mother for a long time until her mother's immigration issue was settled. This struggle is what drove Tammy to fight for reforms in the US immigration system.

Her family struggled with money issues which made her strong so that she could fight her way to a good life. She chose to join the US army as a combat soldier where she became a Black Hawk helicopter pilot. Tammy also completed a Ph.D. in Southeast Asian studies.

In 2004, while she was serving in Kuwait and Iraq, the helicopter she was co-piloting was hit by Iraqi insurgents, and she lost both her legs and some movement one of her arms.

## Payao Poontarat

Payao Poontarat was a Thai boxing legend best known for winning the bronze medal at the 1976 Montreal Olympic Games becoming the first Thai to win any Olympic medal. He became a national treasure despite losing in the semifinals.

He could not participate in the 1980 Moscow Olympics due to a widespread boycott of the event by many of the world countries.

Payao turned professional boxer in late 1981, and his first match was against Tito Abella, a Filipino fighter who had 30 wins under his belt. Even then, Payao defeated him in the second round firmly establishing his place in the professional boxing world. He retired in 1985 after which he joined the police force, and then entered into Thai politics.

However, he was affected by a paralyzing disease which took his life in 2006 at the young age of 46! But we Thais are very proud of this boxing legend's achievements and the accolades he brought to our country.

## Tony Jaa

This highly celebrated Thai actor's real name is Phanom Yeerum. Tony Jaa is an action choreographer, martial artist, director, stuntman, and actor. He was also a Buddhist monk for a while. He was an ardent fan of Bruce Lee, Jet Li, and Jackie Chan films and watched and studied them in detail. He trained in Muay Thai at a local temple since the age of 10.

Tony Jaa started his film career at the age of 15 as a stuntman. He achieved stardom with the famous movie, *Ong-Bak: Muay Thai Warrior*. He continued to do very well in Thai movies and Jackie Chan cast him in *Rush Hour 3*. His recent famous movies include *Furious 7, xXx: Return of Xander Cage,* and *Triple Threat.*

## Kiatisuk Senamuang

Kiatisuk Senamuang is a former football player and coach. He was born on August 11, 1973, in Udon Thani. He played for the national team, and his goal tally was 251 in 339 matches which spanned a career of 18 years. He later served as a coach of the Thailand national football team from 1992 until 2007.

Tony Jaa

# CHAPTER 7
# MAJOR CITIES AND ATTRACTIONS IN THAILAND

Landscape of river in Bangkok cityscape in night time

There are many beautiful cities and islands that you must see during your visit to my fabulous country. Here are some of my favorite places.

## Bangkok

The capital city of Thailand is a must-visit place with a mind-boggling array of things to see and do. Modern architecture and soaring skyscrapers mingle beautifully with amazing museums and art galleries that showcase the rich history of this beautiful city.

You have a multitude of beautiful and ornate Buddhist temples, fantastic floating markets, great street food, huge malls, and gourmet restaurants. You can see Muay Thai fights too. The excellent transport system of Bangkok combines BTS sky trains, buses, MRT subway trains, taxis, and tuk-tuks.

### Fun Fact
Bangkok famously known as the "City of Angels" over the world. It is called so because the Thai name of Bangkok, Krung Thep, translates to 'City of Angels'.

Temple of the Emerald Buddha and Grand Palace

## Grand Palace and Wat Phra Kaew

The Grand Palace has been the home of the Thai kings since it was build in 1782. Its beautiful architecture and intricate designs leave you spellbound. The Wat Phra Kaew is the Royal Buddhist temple within the Grand Palace, and it holds the enchanting and sacred Emerald Buddha. This image of Buddha was carved from a single emerald rock.

Wat Arun — Also known as the Temple of Dawn, Wat Arun is one of the most easily recognizable silhouettes in Bangkok. Built in the ancient Khmer style, the stupa, or dome, has intricate and ornate floral designs.

**Floating Market** — Damnoen Saduak is the pioneer of floating markets in Thailand. You can see rows of wooden boats laden with fresh fruit and vegetables, flowers, and foods floating down the river. Be sure to stop floating vendors and ask them to whip up a yummy meal of noodles or any other dish of your choice.

Other places to see in Bangkok include Chinatown, Wat Pho (which houses the gigantic reclining Buddha), Chao Phraya River, Chatuchak Weekend Market, and Khao San Road. Let me give you some more fascinating information about my capital city:

The official name of Bangkok is *'Krung Thep Mahanakhon Amon Rattanakosin Mahinthara Ayuthaya Mahadilok Phop Noppharat Ratchathani Burirom Udomratchaniwet Mahasathan Amon Piman Awatan Sathit Sakkathattiya Witsanukam Prasit!'* Oh yes, it is! It holds the Guinness Record for the longest name of any given place.

Bangkok is called 'Venice of the East' for having as many canals and waterways as the Italian city.

The Chao Phraya River flows right through the middle of this fascinating capital city.

Koh Larn Island, Pattaya

There are numerous islands off the coast of Pattaya that you can visit and explore. The Nong Nooch Tropical Botanical Gardens, the gigantic Sanctuary of Truth, and Silverlake Vineyard are great places to visit in Pattaya. Here are some more fun things for kids in this city on the eastern coast of Thailand:

**Pattaya** – Although many people mistake Pattaya to be a destination for adults rather than for children, there are many fun things to do and see in this fascinating place. The beaches of Pattaya are gorgeous, and people flock from all over the world to soak in the sun and sand in this beautiful city. You can spend an entire day on one of the beaches and not feel bored at all.

By the way, Pattaya rose into tourist prominence only in the 1980s. Before that, it was not even a city; just a deserted beach. You can reach Pattaya via train from Bangkok. The city is now home to an international airport as well.

**Kombat Group Thailand** – This is a training and fitness camp where you can learn the basics of Muay Thai and show off your newly learned skills to your friends back home.

**Pattaya Sheep Farm** – This sheep farm is the largest one in Thailand and is a great place to spend an entire day. You can see alpacas, Sika deer, and other exotic animals too.

**Ramayana Water Park** – You cannot miss this amazing water park with fun and thrilling water and dry rides fit to blow your mind.

Ramayana Water Park, Pattaya

43

## Phuket

Phuket is Thailand's largest island and is a popular tourist spot. The word Phuket translates to 'mountain jewel.'

Phuket is home to numerous beaches to fit your needs including the Freedom Beach, Karon Beach, Kathu Beach, and of course, the most popular tourist beach, Patong Beach. Promthep Cape offers excellent views of the setting sun. Phuket is home to 36 beaches.

Additionally, you can see world-class Muay Thai fights in Phuket. The food scene is great as well. You can go hiking, interact with elephants, go snorkeling and diving to see the beautiful undersea vistas, and jet ski your way through the beautiful waters surrounding Phuket.

One of the islands of Phuket was used in the Bond movie, The Man with the Golden Gun, after which the island took on the name of James Bond Island. Phuket is also home to a 148-foot Buddha marble statue that offers stunning views of the island.

Although Thailand is home to some of the most exotic and strange non-vegetarian foods, Phuket hosts an annual vegetarian festival which is a huge event attracting many visitors to the island.

### Fun Fact

The most important cultural sites in Phuket are the Big Buddha and Wat Chalong. Can you recall the Thai name for a Buddhist temple? Yes! It's 'Wat.'

Chalong temple

## Ayutthaya

Ayutthaya is a UNESCO World Heritage Site and has a rich history. At one point in time, Ayutthaya was one of the wealthiest and most cosmopolitan cities of the world.

### Fun Fact
Ayutthaya was the capital of Thailand before Bangkok.

Here are some fascinating facts about this historical city of Thailand:

- There are more than 2000 temples in Ayutthaya.
- It was founded in 1350 A.D. by Prince U-Thong of the Ayutthaya Kingdom.
- The Burmese destroyed Ayutthaya in 1767 which resulted in the downfall of the kingdom.

Stone Buddha head entwined in bodhi tree roots

> You must visit Wat Mahathat which has a Buddha head on a tree. Other beautiful temples you must see are Wat Ratchaburana and Wat Phra Si Sanphet.

## Chiang Mai

Chiang Mai has more than 300 temples and is known to be the heart of the Lanna Kingdom which flourished for over 700 years in northern Thailand. Here are some tourist attractions you must not miss in Chiang Mai:

- Chiang Mai Night Zoo
- Hiking in lush green jungles
- Rafting on raging rivers
- Hike or drive to Doi Inthanon, the highest peak in Thailand
- Interact with elephants in a well-maintained and ethical elephant sanctuary
- See stunning waterfalls
- Meet ethnic hill tribes

Chiang Mai is sometimes referred to as Thailand's 'northern capital.' The Songkran festival is celebrated with pomp and fervor in Chiang Mai. Chiang Mai translates to 'New Town.'

# Kanchanaburi

Erawan Falls

Kanchanaburi is also home to many museums dedicated to World War II. This city, located in the west of the country, was founded by King Rama I in the 19th century. When in Kanchanaburi, you must not miss the stunning waterfalls and splendid lakes and caves.

The Erawan National Park in Kanchanaburi houses the multi-level Erawan Falls as well as the Pra That Caves. The Sai Yok National Park is also a great place for a picnic.

**Krabi** — Krabi is made up of more than 80 small islands, surrounded by numerous national parks, and is located at the mouth of the Krabi River. Krabi City is the capital of Krabi Province on the west coast of the south of Thailand. Some of the most important national parks housed in Krabi are Koh Phi Phi National Park, the town of Ao Nang, Railay Beach, and the Hat Noppharat Thara National Park.

## Pop Quiz!

What is the name of the bridge that Kanchanaburi is famous for?

1. The River Kwai Bridge
2. Kanchanaburi Bridge
3. Thailand Bridge

(Answer — 1. The River Kwai Bridge); this bridge was built by the Allied prisoners of war under Japanese supervision. It connected Thailand to Myanmar.

**Koh Phangan** — Koh Phangan is a nature lover's dream. You can see pristine waterfalls, calm and beautiful beaches, and lush green forests. You can find a lot of cooking schools where you will be taught and allowed to make your favorite Thai dishes.

Krabi is the perfect place for you to indulge in outdoor activities like parasailing, snorkeling, kayaking, and bird watching. Koh Phi Phi belongs to Krabi Province and is one of the most picturesque islands of Thailand.

Aerial panoramic view of Koh Hong island, Krabi

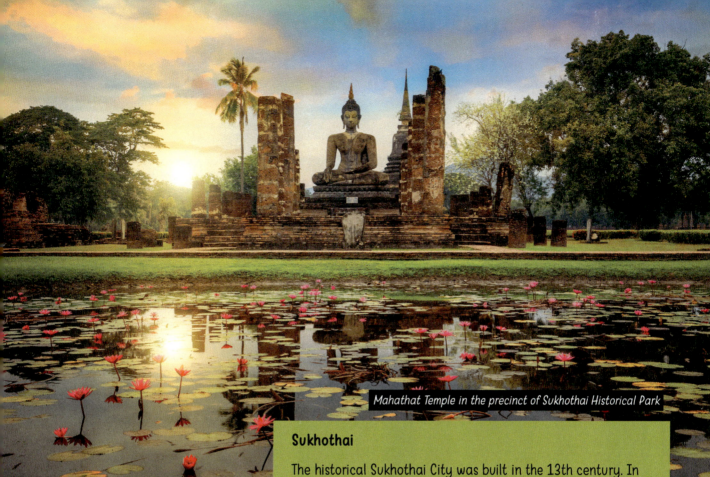

*Mahathat Temple in the precinct of Sukhothai Historical Park*

## Sukhothai

The historical Sukhothai City was built in the 13th century. In fact, it was the first capital of Thailand. You can still see wonderful and glorious ruins that take you back in time. The Sukhothai Historical Park is also a UNESCO World Heritage Site. This city also has numerous religious temples. The other main attractions in this historical city are Ramkhamhaeng National Museum, Royal Palace, Ramkhamhaeng National Park, and Sri Satchanalai National Park.

## Koh Samui

Located in the Thai Gulf, Koh Samui is great for families with some beautifully stunning white, sandy beaches like Mae Nam, Lamai, and Chaweng. You can also visit the old fishing village close by. This island is also home to a strange Buddhist temple that holds a mummified monk. Koh Samui has some outstanding golf courses and exotic beach resorts.

Koh Samui is also famous for its coral reefs and wide vistas of coconut trees lining the stunning beaches. The Buffalo Fighting Festival is also a famous annual event of this charming island.

*Angthong National Marine Park, Koh Samui*

So, that brings us to the end of this fascinating trip across my wondrous country, Thailand. I certainly hope you enjoyed the journey as much as I did. I think it is great to end a learning experience like this Thailand trip with a quiz, and I hope you are ready for it.

But before that, can you answer the following questions to help me understand how much of the trip you enjoyed?

What was the best part of the Thailand journey? Why?

_____
_____
_____
_____
_____

If you got an opportunity to visit my country again, which is the first place you will want to visit again? Why?

_____
_____
_____
_____

Now, for the quiz! I will start with a very simple question.

What is the name of the river that flows through the middle of Bangkok?

1. Mekong River
2. Chao Phraya River
3. Salween River

(Answer – 2. Chao Phraya River)

Which country borders Thailand in the south?

1. China
2. India
3. Malaysia

(Answer – 3. Malaysia)

In which continent is Thailand located?

1. Europe
2. Australia
3. Asia

(Answer – 3. Asia)

What is the primary religion followed in Thailand?

1. Buddhism
2. Christianity
3. Islam

(Answer – 1. Buddhism)

What is the current capital city of Thailand?

1. Ayutthaya
2. Chiang Mai
3. Bangkok

(Answer – 3. Bangkok)

Which city in the north of Thailand translates to 'New Town?'

1. Chiang Rai
2. Chiang Mai
3. Phuket

(Answer – 2. Chiang Mai)

What is the meaning of 'Krung Thep'?'

1. City of Stars
2. City of Beaches
3. City of Angels

(Answer – 3. City of Angels)

What does Thailand translate to in English?

1. The Land of the Free
2. The Land of the Slaves
3. The Land of the Kings

(Answer – 1. The Land of the Free)

What is the official language spoken in Thailand?

1. Thai
2. Chinese
3. English

(Answer – 1. Thai)

What is the currency of Thailand?

1. Dollar
2. Yen
3. Baht

(Answer – 3. Baht)

What is the common English name of the famous Thai dish, Som Tam?

1. Green papaya salad
2. Thailand crepe
3. Mango and sticky rice

(Answer – 1. Green papaya salad)

Which is the largest exported crop of Thailand?

1. Rice
2. Rubber
3. Sugarcane

(Answer – 1. Rice)

What is the national sport of Thailand?

1. Muay Thai
2. Football
3. Golf

(Answer – 1. Muay Thai also known as Thai boxing)

Which country colonized Thailand in the 20th century?

1. Britain
2. France
3. Thailand was never colonized

(Answer – 3. Thailand was never colonized)

What is the name of the famous weekend market close to Bangkok?

1. Chatuchak Weekend Market
2. Bangkok Weekend Market
3. Floating Weekend Market

(Answer – 1. Chatuchak Weekend Market)

On that note, let me say goodbye to you. Hope you have a safe trip back home, and please share your Thailand experiences with your friends there.

I have thoroughly enjoyed this journey through Thailand with you.
Feel free to visit us at www.dinobibi.com and check out our other titles!

## Dinobibi Travel for Kids

## Dinobibi History for Kids

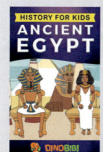 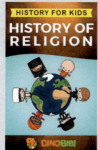 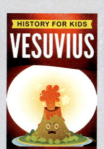  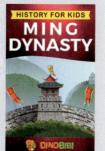
    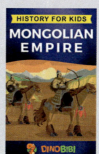 

Made in the USA
Las Vegas, NV
30 March 2023